E·Z Bock's Best

CONTENTS

The original series of
"Outstanding Piano Arrangements of Hymns and Gospel Songs by Fred Bock"

BG0557 BOCK'S BEST Vol I
BG0572 BOCK'S BEST Vol II
BG0679 BOCK'S BEST Vol III
BG0880 BOCK'S BEST Vol IV
BG0941 BOCK'S BEST Vol V

FOREWORD

I distinctly remember my professor coming into a theory class while a student at Anderson University (IN) in the mid 70's, holding up a Fred Bock piano book and telling us we needed to study the harmonic ideas which had been employed in this collection of arrangements. At first it sounded like just another "busy" assignment. But as we began to study the arranging techniques and the ingenious harmonies, it quickly became clear that this was not going to be a "business as usual" theory class. Little did I know that this would be the beginning of a unique and very special connection with Fred Bock.

In the early 80's I submitted a collection of instrumental solos and duets with piano accompaniment which the Fred Bock Music Company accepted for publication. It was one of my very first publications and Fred was particularly helpful in the process of fine-tuning this collection. He was also at times brutally honest, for he wanted this to be a successful publication for grass roots churches, for me as the arranger, and for the Fred Bock Music Company. I learned quickly that he was not only a first-rate professional with a deep compassion for local church musicians, but it was apparent he was a very shrewd businessman as well, attributes which were reaffirmed repeatedly over the years as I contributed to the Fred Bock Music catalogs.

Prior to his untimely death in 1998, I had the opportunity to be with Fred in numerous venues. I saw him operate in workshops, concert settings, and enjoyed interacting with him over the occasional meal or airport run. Each time I benefitted from his tremendous musicianship, depth of wisdom, and marveled at his uncanny and spontaneous wit. Fred had the unique ability to see the sublime in the ordinary. This gift of insight was never more evident than in his piano arrangements. His lush and often unpredictable harmonies gave familiar melodies fresh "new clothing" and provided inspirational backdrops from which familiar and not-so-familiar texts and melodies could spring forth. Over the years, thousands of pianists and worshipers have been the beneficiaries of his unique and inspiring interpretations.

The collection you hold in your hand is the result of an invitation from the Fred Bock Music Company staff to provide a resource by which the Fred Bock legacy could be passed on to subsequent generations of pianists. Based on Fred's arrangements from the *"Bock's Best"* collections, they are simplified renditions of Fred's original settings. These arrangements are particularly suitable for the lesser experienced pianist, whether younger or older. They will also work for the experienced pianist who decides he/she needs something right away with virtually no practice time! (Ever had one of those experiences?) If you are a piano teacher, consider using these arrangements in conjunction with the correlating original from the *"Bock's Best"* series. They can be played at the same time by two pianists--one more advanced, and one not-so-advanced--because they are in the same keys and they maintain the original harmonizations and stylistic interpretations. More than once as I have worked at editing these arrangements, I have felt as if I were treading on holy ground. In Fred's own inimitable style, they are fresh, creative and just plain fun!

If you are a newcomer to the Fred Bock piano arrangements, you will have the same feeling I did in my college theory class as you realize these are not your typical "run-of-the-mill" arrangements. If you are an old friend of Fred's arrangements, I hope you will find these to be accurate and accessible translations of the originals. May they enhance your ministry and lift your spirit! And, in the immortal words of Fred himself, "Make sure you play all the notes!"

Lloyd Larson

Lloyd Larson
Minneapolis, Minnesota
May 2001

GREAT IS THY FAITHFULNESS

WILLIAM M. RUNYAN
Arranged by FRED BOCK
Edited by LLOYD LARSON

17
21
25
Strongly
f
29
33
ten.

37
41
ff
45
3
3
49
53
ten.
pp

MORNING HAS BROKEN

Traditional Gaelic Melody
Arranged by FRED BOCK
Edited by LLOYD LARSON

Moderato (♩ = 120)

21
26
31
36
f
41
mf

46
51
56
61
66
mf
f

71
76
81
86
Ped.
91
R.H.

WHEN I SURVEY THE WONDROUS CROSS

LOWELL MASON
Arranged by FRED BOCK
Edited by LLOYD LARSON

21
25
29
ten.
33
mp
37
41

mf
p
mel.
pp
Ped.

COME, THOU FOUNT OF EVERY BLESSING

JOHN WYETH
Arranged by FRED BOCK
Edited by LLOYD LARSON

17
21
Ped.
25
29
A little slower
mf
mp
33
mp
mf

Bright and crisp
37
mf
41
f
45
Slowing
49
8vb
Both hands 8va
L.H.
ff
R.H.
Ped.

WHAT CHILD IS THIS?

Traditional English Melody
Arranged by FRED BOCK
Edited by LLOYD LARSON

17
21
25
Warmly
f
30
35

39
Ped.
44
Ped.
49
53
58
Slowing
mp
mf
mp
p
pp

THIS OL' HOUSE

STUART HAMBLEN
Arranged by FRED BOCK
Edited by LLOYD LARSON

17
21
25
29
33

37
42
47
51
55
8va
ff
Ped.
8vb

WE GATHER TOGETHER

Netherlands Folk Song
Arranged by FRED BOCK
Edited by LLOYD LARSON

17
mf
21
25
mp
29
33
mp

37
41
45
mf
50
f
54
mp
mel.
mf

58
mel.
mf
62
66
Legato
mp
70
mf
74
L.H.
f
R.H.
rit.
ff
Ped.
Ped.
Ped.
Ped.

HALLE, HALLE, HALLE

Traditional Caribbean Folk Song
Arranged by FRED BOCK
Edited by LLOYD LARSON

*"Hallelujah Chorus" from THE MESSIAH by G. F. Handel

Brightly
legato
mf
f
legato

Brightly
r.h. legato
subito

Broaden
accellerando
ff
rit.
Brightly
(both hands)
8va
r.h.
l.h.
ff

THERE IS A BALM IN GILEAD

Traditional Spiritual
Arranged by FRED BOCK
Edited by LLOYD LARSON

20
24
28
f
32
Ped.
36
Ped.
Ped.
Ped.
39
8va
p
Ped.

ALL FOR JESUS

Anonymous
Arranged by FRED BOCK
Edited by LLOYD LARSON

17
a tempo
ten.
ten.
21
25
29
ten.
ten.
33
f

37
41
ff
45
mf
f
Ped.
49
8va
8va
mf
8va
mp
pp

Fred Bock Music Company